ALIA BONCHEFF

Wine Not?

Fun Quotes and Deliciously Interesting Facts About Wine

First edition

*This book was professionally typeset on Reedsy.
Find out more at reedsy.com*

Contents

1

Introduction

Picture this: You're at a dinner party. The host offers you a glass of wine, and as you take that first glorious sip, someone across the table starts talking about "terroir" and how they can taste the subtle hints of "wet stone" in their glass. You nod, smile, and secretly hope they don't ask for your opinion because, let's be honest, you're just here for a good time and a good drink. Sound familiar?

Welcome to *Wine Not?*—a book that's as much about enjoying wine as it is about understanding it. Whether you're a seasoned sommelier who can detect the difference between a Napa and a Bordeaux in one sniff, or someone who simply picks a bottle based on how pretty the label is, this book is for you. Why? Because wine shouldn't be intimidating. It should be fun, just like the best dinner parties, where the conversation flows as freely as the Cabernet.

Let me introduce myself: I'm someone who's fallen deeply, madly in love with wine. But not in the way you might think. Sure, I've swirled, sniffed, and sipped my way through more wine tastings than I can count, but the real joy I find in wine is in the stories, the history, and yes, even the quirky facts that make it the beloved beverage it is today. I wrote this book because I believe that wine is meant to be enjoyed, celebrated, and shared—and what better way to do that than with a glass in hand and a smile on your face?

We're about to embark on a delightful journey through vine-yards, history, and a few laugh-out-loud moments that might just have you saying, "Wine not?"

But what's a book about wine without a little humor? Scattered throughout these pages are some of the funniest anecdotes and quotes about wine that I've come across over the years. After all, wine has been the muse for poets, artists, and yes, even comedians for centuries. So why not raise a glass, have a laugh, and enjoy the ride?

So, why should you read this book? Because it's not just about wine—it's about enhancing your experience with wine. Whether you're looking to deepen your knowledge, impress at your next dinner party, or simply find a good excuse to open that bottle you've been saving, this book is your perfect companion. By the time you're done reading, you'll not only know more about wine, but you'll also have a newfound appreciation for the stories behind every sip.

As we move into the next chapter, we'll start where all good stories do—at the beginning. The history of wine is as rich and complex as the finest vintage. So grab a glass, get comfortable, and let's dive in. Cheers to a delicious adventure ahead!

2

Wine Through the Ages

The Beginning of Greatness

Let's rewind the clock—way back. I'm talking about 6,000 BC, when your ancestors were just figuring out the whole "civilization" thing. Somewhere in what is now Georgia (the country, not the state), an enterprising group of early humans discovered that if you left some grapes in a pot for a while, something magical happened. That magic, of course, was fermentation, and just like that, wine was born. These early winemakers might not have had the luxury of a sommelier to

6

explain the nuances of their new discovery, but they did know one thing: wine made life a whole lot more interesting.

As time marched on, wine made its way through ancient Persia, Egypt, and Greece, where it became a staple of everyday life. The Egyptians even buried their pharaohs with wine, because, you know, the afterlife is long and you'll need something to pass the time. The Greeks took things a step further, turning wine into a cultural phenomenon. They even had a god of wine, Dionysus, who, let's be honest, probably threw the best parties in all of Olympus.

Along the Way

Wine has come a long way since those ancient days of grape stomping and clay pots. From the vineyards of ancient Persia, wine made its way to Greece, where it became the drink of choice for philosophers, poets, and statesmen alike.

Wine's journey across the globe is nothing short of epic.The Romans took what the Greeks started and perfected it—because, of course, they did. They figured out how to improve vineyards, refine winemaking techniques, and most importantly, how to store and transport wine so that it could be enjoyed by the masses. Ever the empire builders, they took wine with them wherever they went, spreading vineyards across Europe, becoming a key part of daily life and a symbol of civilization itself.

But it wasn't just the Romans who helped spread the love of wine. As trade routes opened up and explorers set sail for new lands, wine traveled with them, finding new homes in far-flung corners of the world. From the sunny vineyards of California to the rugged landscapes of Australia, wine has become a truly global phenomenon, with each region putting its own unique spin on this ancient drink.

But wine didn't just evolve in the vineyard—it also evolved in the glass. Over the centuries, winemakers experimented with different grape varieties, fermentation processes, and aging techniques, leading to the diverse range of wines we know and love today. From the rich, bold reds of Bordeaux to the crisp, refreshing whites of the Loire Valley, wine has continued to evolve, adapting to new tastes, technologies, and trends.

Well Known Wine Lovers

Wine has always had its share of celebrity fans, from kings and queens to artists and philosophers. Cleopatra was known to enjoy a glass (or two) of wine, often sharing it with her lovers in elaborate feasts that have become the stuff of legend. She was no stranger to using wine as a tool of both seduction and diplomacy, perhaps understanding better than most the intoxicating power of a well-poured cup.

Julius Caesar, one of Rome's greatest leaders, was also a fan. He used wine to both celebrate his victories and drown his sorrows (though we imagine there was more of the former than the latter). Caesar's banquets were renowned for their decadence, where the wine flowed as freely as the politics of the time. In a way, wine was as much a part of his strategy as his legions—it eased tensions, sealed alliances, and sometimes even helped to soften the blow of an inevitable betrayal.

Fast forward to the Renaissance, and we find Leonardo da Vinci—yes, that Leonardo—indulging his love for wine in a much more personal way. Between painting masterpieces and inventing the future, da Vinci tended to his very own vineyard.

While we may never know if he was as skilled at winemaking as he was at painting, the mere thought of him sipping on his own vintage while sketching the Mona Lisa is enough to make any wine lover smile. His vineyard, gifted by the Duke of Milan, still exists today, a living testament to his passion for the grape.

Across the pond and a few centuries later, Thomas Jefferson, America's third president, emerged as one of the country's first wine connoisseurs. Jefferson's travels through France ignited a lifelong love affair with wine, leading him to amass a collection that would make any sommelier swoon. He believed wine to be "a necessary of life," and his detailed notes on wine varieties and vintages reveal a man who took his libations as seriously as his politics. Jefferson even tried his hand at growing European grape varietals at his Monticello estate, though with less success than his diplomatic endeavors.

And then there's Winston Churchill, whose love of wine, especially Champagne, was as legendary as his leadership. "Remember, gentlemen, it's not just France we are fighting for, it's Champagne!" he quipped during the dark days of World War II. Churchill's tastes were unapologetically lavish; he once famously declared, "My tastes are simple: I am easily satisfied with the best." Indeed, it's said that he started his day with a glass of Pol Roger and kept the bubbles flowing until bedtime. His wartime resolve may have been fueled as much by his indomitable spirit as by his cellar.

These historical figures, each giants in their own right, found solace, inspiration, and even a bit of mischief in the same drink that we enjoy today. Whether toasting a victory, creating a masterpiece, or simply unwinding after a day of ruling empires, wine has been a steadfast companion to some of the greatest minds and personalities in history. So the next time you pour yourself a glass, remember—you're in excellent company.

Of War and Wine

Wine has inspired art, poetry, and philosophy—but it has also inspired war. Yes, you read that right. Throughout history, there have been conflicts where wine was not just a casualty but a cause, proving that sometimes, the stakes are as high as the alcohol content.

One of the most famous of these was the "War of the Beaujolais," a series of skirmishes in 12th century France between rival lords who fought over control of the region's lucrative vineyards. Picture it: knights in shining armor, swords clashing, all for the control of those precious grapes that would produce the beloved Beaujolais wine. This wasn't just a petty feud; it was a battle over the lifeblood of the region's economy. The vineyards were more than just fields of grapes—they were power, prestige, and prosperity. To control the Beaujolais was to control wealth, influence, and the very identity of the land. The war may have been brief, but it left a lasting mark on the region, embedding the vineyards with a history as rich as the wine they produce.

Then there was the "Champagne Riots" of 1911 in France, when local growers, outraged by new regulations that they felt threatened their livelihoods, took to the streets in protest. This wasn't a gentle, "let's discuss this over a glass of bubbly" kind of affair. No, the growers were incensed by what they saw as the dilution of their Champagne's authenticity—literally. The government's decision to allow grapes from outside the Champagne region to be used in production was seen as an affront to the very soul of the sparkling wine. In response, vineyards were set on fire, barrels were smashed, and entire stocks of Champagne were dumped into rivers, turning the waters into a river of rebellion. The chaos was so severe that the French government had to step in to restore order, a reminder that even something as joyous as Champagne can have a fiercely protective side.

Even in the New World, wine played a role in conflict. During the American Revolution, British troops targeted the wine cellars of wealthy colonists, seeing them as a valuable prize of war. Wine wasn't just a luxury—it was a symbol of status and wealth, and looting it was a way to strike at the heart of the colonial elite. Some of the most famous wine cellars in America were pillaged, their contents shipped back to England as spoils of war. These weren't just any bottles; they were the finest vintages, carefully curated collections that represented years of trade and taste. The loss was more than just a few good bottles— it was a blow to the colonial culture and economy, a reminder that in war, nothing is off limits, not even a good Bordeaux.

And let's not forget the time when the French government ordered the destruction of thousands of liters of wine during World War II to keep it from falling into the hands of the Nazis. Winemakers in Bordeaux and Burgundy, among other regions, were forced to destroy their own stock, pouring it into the streets, rather than let the enemy savor their hard-earned vintages. It was a sacrifice of heritage and pride, a testament to the lengths people will go to protect what they hold dear—even if it means losing something they love.

So, there you have it—the history of wine in all its rich, complex, and sometimes surprising glory. From its humble be-ginnings in ancient clay pots to its role in wars and revolutions, wine has been a constant companion to humanity, shaping cultures and bringing people together—even if sometimes it's through conflict. As we move forward in this book, we'll continue to explore the many facets of wine, from the science of winemaking to the art of tasting, all while keeping things fun, light-hearted, and just a little bit cheeky. Because if history has taught us anything, it's that wine is more than just a drink—it's an experience, a passion, and occasionally, something worth fighting for. I'll drink to that!

Wine Today

Fast forward to the present, and wine has never been more popular—or more diverse. Today, wine is enjoyed by people all around the world, from the bustling streets of New York City to the quiet vineyards of Tuscany. With thousands of grape varieties and countless styles, there's truly a wine for every palate and every occasion.

The wine industry has also embraced innovation, with winemakers experimenting with new techniques and technologies to push the boundaries of what's possible. Organic, biodynamic, and natural wines are on the rise, catering to a growing demand for sustainability and authenticity. Meanwhile, the world of wine has become more accessible than ever, thanks to wine apps, online wine clubs, and a new generation of sommeliers who are more interested in sharing their passion than showing off their knowledge.

But perhaps the most exciting thing about wine today is how it continues to evolve and adapt to changing tastes and trends. Whether you're a fan of bold, full-bodied reds or crisp, refreshing whites, there's always something new to discover in the world of wine. And as more people become interested in learning about and enjoying wine, the culture of wine is becoming more inclusive, welcoming everyone to join in the fun.

3

How Wine is Made

Ever wonder how that bottle of wine sitting on your table went from a bunch of grapes on a vine to the delicious drink in your glass? Well, you're in for a treat. Making wine is both an art and a science, a process that's as old as civilization itself yet still full of mystery and magic. In this chapter, we'll take a journey from the vineyard to the cellar, uncovering the secrets behind how wine is made. So, grab a glass, and let's dive in!

The Grapes

Not all grapes are created equal. In fact, the journey to a great

15

wine starts long before the grapes are even harvested. The type of grape, the soil it's grown in, the temperature, and the weather all play crucial roles in shaping the final product.

Let's start with the grapes. Different grape varieties have their own unique characteristics, from the thick-skinned, bold Cabernet Sauvignon to the delicate, floral Riesling. But it's not just the grape variety that matters—it's also where and how it's grown.

The soil, or "terroir" as the French like to call it, is the foundation of the vineyard. Some soils retain more water, while others drain quickly, and these differences can dramatically affect the flavor of the grapes. For example, grapes grown in limestone-rich soils tend to produce wines with bright acidity, while those from volcanic soils often have a distinct minerality.

Then there's the climate. Warm temperatures can lead to riper, sweeter grapes, which means higher sugar levels and, ultimately, higher alcohol content in the wine. Cooler climates, on the other hand, tend to produce grapes with higher acidity and more complex flavors. But it's not just about temperature—weather events like frost, hail, and even too much rain can make or break a vintage, affecting everything from the size of the grapes to their sugar content.

In short, winemaking starts in the vineyard, and a good winemaker knows how to work with the grapes they're given, coaxing out their best qualities to create a wine that's a true expression of its origins.

The Harvest

Every bottle of wine starts with a harvest, but not all harvests are created equal. So how do winemakers—and wine lovers—know when a harvest is good or bad?

A good harvest is all about balance. The grapes need to be ripe but not overripe, with enough sugar to create a well-balanced wine but still retaining enough acidity to give the wine freshness and structure. Weather plays a huge role here—too much rain can dilute the flavors, while too much heat can lead to overly sweet, flabby wines.

Winemakers often talk about the "vintage," which is simply the year the grapes were harvested. Some vintages are legendary, producing wines that can age for decades, while others are less memorable. But even in a less-than-stellar vintage, a skilled winemaker can still produce great wine by carefully selecting the best grapes and using their expertise to make the most of what they've got.

So, the next time you're in the wine aisle, take a look at the vintage and remember: a good harvest can make all the difference.

The Art of Making Wine

Once the grapes are harvested, the real magic begins. The journey from grape to glass is a complex process, but at its core, it's about transforming the fruit of the vine into something much more delicious. Here's a quick rundown of how it's done.

First, the grapes are crushed to release their juice—a step that used to be done by foot but is now mostly handled by machines. For white wine, the grape skins are usually removed right away, while for red wine, they're left in to give the wine its color and tannins.

Next comes fermentation. Fermentation is where the magic happens. It's the moment when grape juice turns into wine, thanks to the power of yeast. But what exactly is fermentation, and why is it so important?

In simple terms, fermentation is the process by which yeast converts the sugars in grape juice into alcohol and carbon dioxide. But there's a lot more to it than that. The type of yeast used, the temperature of the fermentation, and even the length of time it takes can all influence the final flavor of the wine.

For red wines, fermentation usually takes place in large open vats, allowing the grape skins to stay in contact with the juice and impart their color and tannins. White wines, on the other hand, are often fermented in closed tanks, which helps preserve their fresh, fruity flavors.

Some wines undergo a secondary fermentation called malo-lactic fermentation, which converts the tart malic acid in the wine into softer, creamier lactic acid. This process is what gives some Chardonnays their characteristic buttery flavor.

Fermentation is both an art and a science, and it's where the winemaker's skill really comes into play. By carefully controlling the conditions of fermentation, they can coax out the best flavors from the grapes and create a wine that's truly unique.

After fermentation, the wine is often aged to allow the flavors to develop further. This can be done in stainless steel tanks, which preserve the wine's freshness, or in oak barrels, which can add complex flavors like vanilla, spice, and toast. The aging process can take anywhere from a few months to several years, depending on the style of wine the winemaker is aiming for.

Finally, the wine is bottled and—voilà!—it's ready to be enjoyed. But as you can see, there's a lot that goes into that bottle before it ever reaches your table.

4

Grape Varietals and Wine Regions

Wine is like a passport to the world, taking you on a journey through different countries, climates, and cultures—all without leaving your seat. In this chapter, we're going to explore the vast and varied world of grape varietals and the regions that make them famous. From the sun-drenched vineyards of California to the rolling hills of Tuscany, every wine tells a story of its origin. So, let's uncork the globe and see what's inside.

Wine Regions of the World

Wine is made in just about every corner of the world, but there are a few regions that stand out as the crème de la crème. These are the places where the combination of climate, soil, and tradition come together to create wines that are nothing short of spectacular.

Let's start in France, the undisputed king of wine regions. Bordeaux, Burgundy, and Champagne are just a few of the names that have become synonymous with the best wine in the world. Each region has its own unique terroir, producing wines with distinctive flavors and characteristics. In Bordeaux, for example, you'll find rich, full-bodied reds made from Cabernet Sauvignon and Merlot, while Burgundy is famous for its elegant Pinot Noirs and Chardonnays.

But France isn't the only game in town. Italy is another heavyweight, with regions like Tuscany and Piedmont leading the charge. Tuscany, with its rolling hills and cypress-lined roads, is home to Chianti, a red wine made primarily from Sangiovese grapes. Chianti is a wine that sings of its rustic roots—think vibrant red fruit, earthy undertones, and a touch of acidity that makes it the perfect partner for a hearty Italian meal. Then there's Piedmont, a region that produces some of the most powerful and complex wines in the world. Barolo and Barbaresco, made from the Nebbiolo grape, are wines that demand attention. They're bold, with flavors of tar, roses, and truffles, and a tannic structure that can stand the test of time. These are wines that reward patience, revealing their full glory only after years of careful aging.

Cross the Atlantic, and you'll find California's Napa Valley, where the warm, sunny climate produces some of the world's best Cabernet Sauvignon. Napa Valley is a place where in-novation meets tradition, where winemakers are as likely to experiment with new techniques as they are to honor the tried-and-true methods of the past. The result? Wines that are lush, fruit-forward, and incredibly approachable, yet with enough complexity to keep even the most seasoned wine lover intrigued. A glass of Napa Cab is like a taste of California sunshine—rich, ripe, and full of life.

Australia's Barossa Valley is another must-visit on the global wine map, known for its bold, spicy Shiraz. The wines from this region are as big and bold as the landscape itself, with flavors of blackberry, pepper, and sometimes a hint of smoky meat. Barossa Shiraz is the kind of wine that doesn't just accompany a meal—it commands it, standing up to the richest of dishes with its full-bodied intensity.

And let's not forget Spain's Rioja, where Tempranillo reigns supreme. Rioja wines are a study in balance, with flavors of red berries, leather, and vanilla from the oak aging process. These are wines that can be enjoyed young, with their vibrant fruitiness, or aged to develop a more complex, mellow character. The best Riojas are a testament to the art of aging, where time in the bottle transforms the wine into something truly special.

Argentina's Mendoza region is the birthplace of Malbec, a grape that has found its spiritual home in the high-altitude vineyards nestled at the foot of the Andes. Malbec from Mendoza is rich and robust, with flavors of dark fruit, chocolate, and sometimes a touch of floral notes. It's a wine that embodies the rugged beauty of the Argentine landscape, with a structure that's both powerful and smooth, making it a favorite for those who enjoy a bit of intensity in their glass.

These are just a few of the world's top wine regions, each with its own unique story to tell. Whether you're sipping a crisp Sauvignon Blanc from New Zealand's Marlborough, where the wines are known for their zesty acidity and notes of tropical fruit, or a robust Zinfandel from California, which often boasts bold flavors of blackberry, spice, and sometimes a touch of chocolate, you're tasting the history and tradition of the land where it was made.

In each glass of wine, there's a journey waiting to be explored—a journey through vineyards, across continents, and back through centuries of winemaking tradition. As you uncork these stories, you'll discover that wine is not just a drink; it's a global experience, a connection to the places and people who have cultivated this ancient art. So, here's to the wine regions of the world, where every bottle is a passport to adventure, and every sip is a step deeper into the rich tapestry of wine's endless variety.

The Basic Red Wine Varietals

When it comes to red wine, there's a whole spectrum of flavors, from light and fruity to dark and brooding. But no matter what your preference, there's a red wine out there with your name on it.

Let's start with Cabernet Sauvignon, the king of red wines. Known for its bold flavors of blackcurrant, cedar, and tobacco, Cabernet Sauvignon is a full-bodied wine that ages beautifully, developing complex layers of flavor over time. It's the star of Bordeaux, but you'll also find excellent examples from California, Chile, and Australia.

Next up is Merlot, Cabernet's softer, more approachable cousin. With its lush flavors of plum, chocolate, and black cherry, Merlot is a crowd-pleaser that pairs well with just about anything. It's a key player in Bordeaux blends but also shines on its own in places like California and Washington State.

Then there's Pinot Noir, the diva of the wine world. Pinot Noir is notoriously difficult to grow, but when done right, it produces some of the most elegant and nuanced wines in the world. With flavors of red fruit, earth, and spice, Pinot Noir is light in body but big on flavor. It's the signature grape of Burgundy, but you'll also find excellent examples from Oregon, New Zealand, and California's Sonoma Coast.

Other notable red wines include Syrah (or Shiraz, as it's known in Australia), a bold, peppery wine with flavors of blackberry and smoked meat, and Zinfandel, a fruit-forward wine with notes of raspberry, cherry, and spice that's practically synonymous with California.

The Basic White Wine Varietals

White wine might not have the same cachet as red, but it's every bit as diverse and delicious. From crisp and refreshing to rich and creamy, there's a white wine for every palate and occasion.

Chardonnay is the most famous of the white wines, and for good reason. With its rich, buttery flavors of apple, pear, and vanilla, Chardonnay is a versatile wine that can be made in a variety of styles, from crisp and unoaked to full-bodied and barrel-aged. Burgundy is its spiritual home, but you'll find great Chardonnays from California, Australia, and beyond.

If you prefer something a little lighter, Sauvignon Blanc is your go-to. Known for its zesty flavors of lime, green apple, and freshly cut grass, Sauvignon Blanc is a high-acid wine that's perfect for warm weather. It's the signature grape of New Zealand's Marlborough region, but you'll also find great examples from France's Loire Valley and California.

Then there's Riesling, a wine that ranges from bone-dry to lusciously sweet. With its bright acidity and flavors of citrus, peach, and honey, Riesling is one of the most food-friendly wines out there. It's a staple in Germany, but you'll also find excellent Rieslings from Alsace, France, and Washington State.

Other notable white wines include Pinot Grigio, a light, easy-drinking wine with flavors of lemon and green apple, and Viognier, a full-bodied wine with lush, aromatic notes of peach, apricot, and floral.

Rosé

Rosé is the ultimate summer wine, but its appeal goes far beyond the warm months. Made from red grapes that are given just a short time to soak with their skins, rosé has a light, refreshing flavor that's perfect for sipping on its own or pairing with a wide range of foods.

The flavors of rosé can vary widely depending on the grape variety used and the region it comes from. Provençal rosé, made from grapes like Grenache, Syrah, and Cinsault, is typically light, dry, and full of flavors like strawberry, melon, and citrus. In contrast, rosé from Spain, known as rosado, is often a bit darker and fuller-bodied, with flavors of cherry and plum.

No matter what style you prefer, rosé is a versatile wine that's perfect for any occasion. It's a great match for salads, seafood, and light pasta dishes, but it's also delicious on its own as an aperitif.

Champagne

No discussion of wine would be complete without a mention of

Champagne, the sparkling wine that has become synonymous with celebration. But Champagne is more than just a party drink—it's a complex, meticulously crafted wine that requires skill and precision to make.

Champagne comes from the Champagne region of France, where it's made using a traditional method known as méthode champenoise. The process starts with a blend of grapes—usually Chardonnay, Pinot Noir, and Pinot Meunier—which are fermented into a still wine. The wine is then bottled with a small amount of sugar and yeast, which triggers a second fermentation in the bottle. This fermentation produces carbon dioxide, which gets trapped in the bottle and creates those famous bubbles.

But making Champagne isn't just about the bubbles. The wine is aged on its lees (dead yeast cells) for several years, which gives it its characteristic toasty, nutty flavors. After aging, the bottles are carefully turned and tilted—a process known as riddling—to collect the sediment in the neck of the bottle, which is then removed in a process called disgorgement. Finally, the wine is topped up with a small amount of sweetened wine, known as dosage, before being corked and labeled.

The result is a wine that's crisp, effervescent, and perfect for toasting to life's special moments. And while Champagne is the most famous sparkling wine, other regions around the world produce their own versions, like Italy's Prosecco and Spain's Cava, each with its own unique character and style.

Unique and Interesting Grape Varietals

I have an almost embarrassing amount of passion and joy when it comes to drinking a glass of wine. Whether I'm curled up with a good book, hanging out with friends, or just trying to unwind after a long day, there's something about that first sip that just makes everything a little bit better. But here's the thing I love most about wine: every time you pop open a bottle you've never tried before, it's like diving headfirst into a brand-new adventure for your senses. It's a thrill, like finding out your favorite author just released a new book or discovering a hidden gem of a restaurant in your neighborhood.

And let me tell you, I get ridiculously excited when I stumble across a new and interesting wine varietal I haven't tried yet. It's like finding a new favorite show to binge-watch—suddenly, the world is full of possibilities! So, if you're anything like me and love trying something new and exciting, you're in for a treat. I've rounded up some fun and lesser-known wine varietals that have completely stolen my heart, and I'm pretty sure they're going to steal yours too. So grab a glass, and let's dive into this delicious adventure together!

Cinsault (*Pronounced sin-so*) is like that charming underdog you root for in a feel-good movie—the one that sneaks up on you with a smile and wins your heart before you even realize it. It's one of those minor grapes found in Rhône blends and Provençal rosés, usually hanging out in the background, but when it steps into the spotlight, it delivers fresh, punchy reds that are as floral as they are fruity. Picture yourself on a sun-drenched patio, surrounded by the scent of blooming flowers and the taste of ripe red berries, and you've got the essence of Cinsault.

The first time I tried this little gem of a wine, I was hiking the Zinfandel Trail in California. Yes, that's right—a trail named after wine that leads you to more wine. If there's a better way to end a hike than by enjoying a glass of vino, I have yet to discover it. After huffing and puffing my way up the trail, I found myself at a winery (because, of course, I did), where I was introduced to Cinsault. It's a lighter red, the kind that's perfect for a warm day, and I've even been known to chill it slightly when the sun is really beating down. I know all you wine snobs out there are probably shaking your heads at me right now, but hey—when it's hot, a girl's gotta do what a girl's gotta do. And trust me, a slightly chilled Cinsault is a summer game-changer.

Viognier *(Pronounced vee-own-yay)* is the wine equivalent of that friend who always smells amazing, no matter what. You know the one—their scent just floats around them like a fragrant cloud of peaches, tangerines, and honeysuckle. Originating from southern France, this full-bodied white wine is beloved for its perfumed aromas that make you want to close your eyes and just breathe it in.

But Viognier isn't just a pretty face (or nose, as it were). When it's oak-aged, this wine takes on a rich, creamy taste with hints of vanilla that make you wonder how something so elegant can also be so indulgent. It's like having dessert before dinner, and I'm here for it. Whether you're sipping it on a warm evening as the sun sets or pairing it with a creamy pasta dish, Viognier is the wine that makes every moment feel a little more special.

Malvasia Bianca *(Pronounced malvaˈziːa bee-on-ka)* is like the ultimate summer romance—bright, fresh, and just a little bit sweet. This versatile grape can swing both ways, producing wines that are either dry or sweet, but no matter the style, it always brings something fun to the table. Notes of flowers, ripe stone fruit, tropical fruit, and citrus make Malvasia Bianca a wine that practically sings of sunshine and warm breezes. And if you're lucky, you might even catch a hint of those juicy summertime melons that we all crave when the weather heats up.

I first tasted this delightful wine at a California winery, where the owner told me that their Malvasia grape vines came all the way from their ancestral family home in Croatia. That little nugget of information made each sip feel like a mini vacation, whisking me away to a place where the sun shines a little brighter and life moves a little slower. Whether you're enjoying it by the pool or on a picnic, Malvasia Bianca is the wine that's destined to be your new warm-weather favorite.

Teroldego (*Pronounced teh-RAHL-deh-go*) is like the mysterious stranger in a romance novel—dark, brooding, and absolutely irresistible. This high-quality grape variety hails almost exclusively from Trentino, the southern half of Italy's most northerly wine region. With aromas of red berries, dried fruits, and violets, Teroldego lures you in with a promise of something a little different, a little intriguing.

And it doesn't disappoint. The flavors follow through with cherry, cranberry, blackberry, and plum, all wrapped up with a refreshing bitter almond note on the finish. It's the kind of wine that makes you sit up and take notice, leaving you with a taste that lingers long after the glass is empty. Teroldego isn't for the faint of heart—it's bold, complex, and just a little bit enigmatic. But if you're ready to embrace your inner wine adventurer, this is the grape that will take you on a journey you won't soon forget.

5

Wine Tasting

In this chapter, you'll learn how to master the art of wine tasting, from the first swirl to the final sip. We'll cover the essential techniques to properly taste wine, how to identify and appreciate its aromas and flavors, and how to determine if a wine is truly good. Plus, we'll share some of the most exciting and enjoyable places around the world to indulge in wine tasting. By the end, you'll have the confidence to taste wine with flair and know exactly what to look for in every glass.

The Joy of Wine Tasting

Tasting wine is an experience for all your senses, not just your taste buds. To truly appreciate a wine, you need to engage with it fully, from the moment it's poured into your glass to the last lingering sip. Here's a step-by-step guide to tasting wine like a pro:

- **Look**: Before you even take a sip, take a good look at the wine in your glass. Hold it up to the light or against a white background and observe its color and clarity. Is it a deep, inky red, or a pale, translucent white? The color can give you clues about the wine's age and grape variety. For example, red wines often get lighter as they age, while white wines may turn more golden.
- **Swirl**: Gently swirl the wine in your glass. This isn't just for show—it helps to release the wine's aromas by exposing it to air. As the wine coats the sides of the glass, you might notice "legs" or "tears" forming as it trickles back down. Contrary to popular belief, these aren't an indicator of quality but rather of alcohol content and viscosity.
- **Smell**: Next, give the wine a good sniff. Stick your nose right into the glass and inhale deeply. What do you smell? Wine aromas can range from fruity and floral to earthy and spicy. Try to pick out individual scents like berries, citrus, vanilla, or even more unusual notes like leather or tobacco. The more you practice, the better you'll get at identifying these aromas.
- **Sip**: Now for the best part—take a sip! But don't just gulp it down. Let the wine roll over your tongue and take note of the flavors. How does it taste compared to how it smells? You might notice new flavors or subtleties that weren't apparent on the nose. Pay attention to the wine's body (is it

light, medium, or full?), its sweetness, acidity, and tannins (the astringent, mouth-drying sensation, especially in red wines).

- **Swallow (or Spit)**: Professional wine tasters often spit out the wine, especially if they're tasting many wines in one sitting. But for most of us, swallowing is the preferred option—after all, we're here to enjoy the wine! As you swallow, take note of the finish. Does the flavor linger on your palate, or does it fade quickly? A long, complex finish is often a sign of a high-quality wine.
- **Reflect**: Finally, take a moment to reflect on the wine. Did you enjoy it? What stood out to you? Would you drink it again? Every bottle of wine tells a story, and part of the joy of tasting is discovering that story for yourself.

By following these steps, you'll not only get more enjoyment out of each glass but also start to develop a deeper understanding and appreciation for the wide world of wine. Cheers to tasting like a pro!

The Smell of Wine

The aroma of wine is like its calling card—it gives you the first hints of what's to come before you even take a sip. In the world of wine tasting, the smell (or "nose") of a wine is just as important as its taste, and sometimes even more revealing. Here's how to fully appreciate the bouquet of a wine and what it can tell you.

Why Smell Matters: Our sense of smell is incredibly powerful and closely linked to our sense of taste. In fact, much of what we perceive as taste actually comes from smell. When you sniff a glass of wine, you're not just identifying individual scents—you're also setting the stage for how the wine will taste on your palate.

Common Wine Aromas: Different wines have different characteristic aromas. For instance:

- **Red Wines**: Often feature aromas of dark fruits like blackberry, cherry, and plum, along with spices, leather, and sometimes chocolate or coffee.
- **White Wines**: Tend to have lighter, fresher aromas like citrus, apple, pear, and floral notes, along with honey, vanilla, and sometimes minerality.
- **Rosé Wines**: Typically offer a mix of red fruit aromas, like strawberry and raspberry, along with floral and citrus notes.
- **Sparkling Wines**: Often have crisp, fruity aromas with hints of brioche, almond, or yeast, thanks to the aging process.

Developing Your Nose: The more you practice smelling wine, the better you'll get at identifying its aromas. One fun way to train your nose is to smell everything—fruits, flowers, spices, herbs, even the earth after it rains. The broader your scent vocabulary, the easier it will be to pick up on those subtle notes in your glass.

Smelling wine is more than just a step in the tasting process—it's an experience in itself. Each sniff offers a new layer of complexity and a deeper connection to the wine in your glass. So the next time you pour yourself a glass, take a moment to truly breathe it in. You might just discover something new. Cheers!

The Taste of Wine

Tasting wine is where all the elements come together—sight, smell, and, finally, taste. But tasting wine isn't just about the flavor; it's about understanding the different sensations that a wine can offer, from the initial sip to the lingering finish. Here's how to break down the experience of tasting wine and what to look for in each sip.

First Impressions: When you take that first sip of wine, let it coat your entire palate. Notice the immediate flavors that jump out at you. Are they fruity, spicy, or perhaps earthy? These initial flavors give you the first hint of the wine's character.

The Basic Tastes: Wine engages your palate through the basic tastes—sweet, sour, bitter, and sometimes salty:

- **Sweetness**: The first taste to register is often sweetness, especially in wines with residual sugar, like Rieslings or dessert wines. But even in dry wines, you might detect a slight sweetness from the fruit.
- **Acidity**: This is what gives wine its freshness and crispness, making your mouth water. Higher acidity is common in white wines like Sauvignon Blanc and sparkling wines. It balances sweetness and gives the wine a zesty edge.
- **Tannins**: Tannins are the compounds that give red wines their structure and astringency. You'll feel them more than taste them, as they create a drying sensation in your mouth. Tannins come from the grape skins, seeds, and oak barrels, and they're more prominent in wines like Cabernet Sauvignon and Syrah.
- **Bitterness**: While not always present, a slight bitterness can be a part of the wine's profile, especially in wines with

35

high tannins or those aged in oak.

- **Alcohol**: You might also sense the warmth of alcohol, particularly in higher-alcohol wines. This can add body and depth but should be balanced and not overwhelming.

Body: The body of a wine refers to its weight or mouthfeel. Think of it as the difference between skim milk (light-bodied) and whole milk (full-bodied). Wines with higher alcohol, sugar, and tannins tend to have a fuller body. Chardonnay, for example, often has a creamy, full-bodied texture, while Pinot Grigio is usually lighter and crisper.

Flavor Profile: As you continue to taste the wine, try to identify the specific flavors. Are they similar to what you smelled earlier? You might find that some flavors are more pronounced on the palate than on the nose. For example, a wine that smells of fresh berries might taste more like dried fruit, or a wine with floral aromas might reveal more citrus on the palate.

Balance: A well-made wine should have a sense of balance. This means that no single element—sweetness, acidity, tannins, alcohol—should overpower the others. Instead, they should work together harmoniously, creating a cohesive tasting experience. Wines that arc too acidic can taste sharp or sour, while those that are too tannic can be harsh and bitter. The best wines find that perfect balance, making them enjoyable from the first sip to the last.

Finish: The finish is the impression that lingers after you swallow the wine. A long, complex finish is often a sign of a high-quality wine. Pay attention to the flavors that remain and how long they last. Do they fade quickly, or do they evolve and continue to reveal new notes? A wine with a long finish will leave a lasting impression, making you want to go back for another sip.

Developing Your Palate: Tasting wine is a skill that improves with practice. The more wines you taste, the more you'll start to notice the subtle differences and nuances between them. Don't be afraid to take notes, compare wines, and discuss your impressions with others. The key is to taste mindfully, paying attention to each sensation and flavor.

The taste of wine is a journey that takes you through layers of flavor, texture, and complexity. By understanding and appreciating these elements, you'll deepen your enjoyment of every glass and discover a whole new world of wine. So, take your time, savor each sip, and enjoy the delicious adventure. Cheers!

How Can You Tell If A Wine is Good or Not?

When it comes to judging whether a wine is good or not, opinions can be as varied as the wines themselves. But honestly, the answer is simple, and it's best summed up by a wise quote told to me by a wonderful man and fellow wine enthusiast :

"It doesn't matter where it comes from, who makes it, or how much it costs. If you like it, it's good!"- **Jeffrey Smith**

And there you have it! When it comes down to it, the best wine is the one that makes you happy, whether it's a fancy vintage or a bottle you picked up on a whim. So trust your taste buds and enjoy what you love.

Corked Wine: What It Is and How to Spot It

Ah, corked wine—the two words no wine lover wants to hear. But what exactly does it mean when a wine is "corked," and how can you tell if your bottle has fallen victim to this unfortunate fate?

What Is Corked Wine?

Corked wine is a term used to describe a bottle of wine that has been contaminated with a compound called TCA (2,4,6-Trichloroanisole). TCA forms when natural fungi come into contact with certain chlorides found in bleaches and other sanitizing agents used during the cork production process. This compound can taint the wine, rendering it undrinkable. The good news? Corked wine isn't harmful to your health—it's just not going to taste very good.

How to Spot a Corked Wine

Corked wine has a very distinctive smell and taste that's hard to miss once you know what you're looking for:

- **The Smell**: The most telling sign of a corked wine is the smell. It's often described as musty, like wet cardboard, damp basement, or even a soggy old newspaper. If you take a whiff of your wine and it smells off, that's a big red flag.
- **The Taste**: If the wine doesn't smell right, the taste is likely to be off as well. Corked wine will taste flat, dull, and lacking in the usual vibrant fruit flavors you'd expect. It might even

have an unpleasant, moldy aftertaste. Essentially, it tastes as bad as it smells.

- **Appearance**: In most cases, a corked wine will look just like any other bottle of wine—it's the smell and taste that give it away. However, if the cork itself looks moldy or crumbly when you remove it, that might be another indicator that something's amiss.

While encountering a corked wine is never fun, knowing how to identify it and what to do about it can save you from a disappointing experience. And the silver lining? It gives you an excuse to open another bottle! I'll drink to that!

6

Wine Humor and Culture

Wine has a way of bringing out the wit and humor in people, whether it's through clever quotes or memorable stories that make us laugh out loud. In this chapter, we're diving into the lighter side of wine, exploring the quips and anecdotes that have made wine not just a drink, but a source of joy and amusement for centuries. From the vineyard to the dinner table, wine has inspired countless moments of humor, and we've gathered some of the best for your enjoyment.

Silly Wine Tales

Let's start with a classic story from the world of wine that perfectly illustrates how this beloved beverage can turn even the most serious moments into something worth laughing about.

The French Wine Heist: In 2017, a group of daring thieves in France pulled off what could only be described as a "grape" escape. They managed to steal over 300 bottles of some of the world's finest wines from a private cellar in Paris. The total value of the stolen wine? Nearly half a million euros. But here's the kicker: the thieves didn't just break in and grab the bottles. No, they tunneled their way into the cellar from the catacombs beneath the city—a feat that took weeks of planning. While the crime was certainly serious, the image of wine-loving bandits channeling their inner Oceans 11 made headlines around the world and left many people chuckling at the audacity of the plot.

The Toast Gone Wrong: At a fancy dinner party in New York, a well-meaning host decided to impress their guests by opening a rare bottle of wine—a vintage Bordeaux that had been carefully aging in their cellar for decades. As they poured the wine and raised their glass to toast, they proudly proclaimed, "To life, love, and this exquisite bottle of wine!" Unfortunately, as the guests took their first sip, it became clear that something was very, very wrong. The wine had long since passed its prime and tasted more like vinegar than vintage. The host's face turned as red as the wine, but the guests, being good sports, laughed it off, turning a potential disaster into a memorable moment.

The Mystery of the Disappearing Wine: In a small Italian village, there was once a vineyard known for its incredible wine, made from a rare and ancient grape variety. Each year, the winemaker would bottle just a few hundred bottles, selling them to locals and tourists alike. But one year, something strange happened. Despite the vineyard producing the usual amount of grapes, the wine production was mysteriously low. Bottles that were supposed to be full were suddenly empty. The winemaker was baffled until one night, he decided to stake out the cellar. What he found was not a thief, but his own dog, who had developed a taste for fine wine and had been uncorking the bottles one by one. The winemaker couldn't be too mad—after all, it was clear the dog had excellent taste.

The Wine Auction Surprise: At a high-profile wine auction, a bidder was determined to secure a bottle of one of the rarest wines in the world, a 1945 Romanée-Conti. The bidding war was intense, with prices skyrocketing higher and higher. When the final bid was accepted at an eye-watering $558,000, the room erupted in applause. But the moment of victory was short-lived—after the auctioneer declared the winner, the bidder realized that they had misread the lot number and had intended to bid on a completely different bottle. The room fell silent before laughter broke out, and the flustered bidder had to sheepishly explain the mix-up, proving that even the most seasoned wine collectors can have their off days.

Fun Quotes about Wine

Wine has also been the subject of countless quotes that capture its essence, its charm, and its undeniable ability to make life a little bit more enjoyable. Here are some of our favorites:

"I cook with wine, sometimes I even add it to the food." — **W.C. Fields**

"Age is just a number. It's totally irrelevant unless, of course, you happen to be a bottle of wine." — **Joan Collins**

"Wine makes daily living easier, less hurried, with fewer tensions and more tolerance." - **Benjamin Franklin**

"As long as we have wine, family holidays will be fine." - **Unknown**

"Wine is bottled poetry." – **Robert Louis Stevenson**

"Wine—because no great story ever started with a salad." - **Unknown**

"My only regret in life is that I did not drink more wine." – **Ernest Hemingway**

"A bottle of wine contains more philosophy than all the books in the world." – **Louis Pasteur**

"What wine goes with Captain Crunch?" – **George Carlin**

"Wine is the most civilized thing in the world." – **Ernest Hemingway**

"Gentlemen, in the little moment that remains to us between the crisis and the catastrophe, we may as well drink a glass of Champagne." – **Paul Claudel**

"The best way to learn about wine is by drinking." **Alexis Lichine**

"Wine is the answer, but I can't remember the question." - **Unknown**

"Beer is made by men, wine by God." — **Martin Luther**

"A day without wine is like...just kidding, I have no idea." - **Anonymous** (taken from the t- shirt I'm currently wearing)

"Penicillin cures, but wine makes people happy." — **Alexander Fleming** (Who knew the discoverer of penicillin also appreciated a good glass of wine?)

"Men are like wine—some turn to vinegar, but the best improve with age." — **Pope John XXIII**

"If food is the body of good living, wine is its soul." – **Clifton Fadiman**

"Wine improves with age. The older I get, the better I like it." — **Anonymous**

"In victory, you deserve Champagne. In defeat, you need it." - **Napoleon Bonaparte**

"Making good wine is a skill; making fine wine is an art." – **Robert Mondavi**

"Today's forecast: sunny with a chance of wine." - **Unknown**

"And wine can of their wits the wise beguile, make the sage frolic, and the serious smile." – **Alexander Pope**

"Time to be a hero and rescue some wine trapped in a bottle." – **Unknown**

"wine cheers the sad, revives the old, inspires the young, makes *weariness forget his toil."* - **Lord Byron**

"With wine and hope, anything is possible." - **Spanish proverb**

"Age and glasses of wine should never be counted." - **Italian proverb**

"You only live once—so drink great wine." - **Anonymous**

"Where there is no wine there is no love." - **Euripides**

The Lighter Side of Wine Culture

Finally, let's not forget the lighter side of wine culture itself— the moments when wine lovers let their hair down and embrace the joy of a good glass (or bottle) of wine.

Wine Tasting with a Twist: In one famous wine-tasting event, the organizer decided to add a little twist to the traditional tasting notes. Instead of describing the wines in the usual way, they decided to write the tasting notes as if they were personal ads. "Tall, dark, and handsome, with a hint of spice and a smooth finish. Looking for a dinner companion who appreciates the finer things in life." Needless to say, the guests had a blast, and the wines were enjoyed with a lot of laughter.

The Wine Workout: A fitness enthusiast who didn't want to miss out on their wine time came up with the idea of the "Wine Workout." The concept? Perform a series of exercises while holding a glass of wine. Squats while sipping, lunges while lifting the glass—by the end of the workout, participants had enjoyed a good sweat and a good wine, though the effectiveness of this workout routine remains debatable.

The Wine Cork Collector: In a quaint little town, a local wine enthusiast had a quirky hobby—collecting wine corks. But this wasn't just any collection. Over the years, the collector had amassed tens of thousands of corks, enough to fill an entire room in their house. Visitors were often treated to a tour of the "Cork Room," where the walls, ceiling, and floor were lined with corks from all over the world. When asked why they started the collection, the enthusiast simply replied, "Well, I had to do something with all those corks!" It became a local attraction, and people would bring corks from their travels to add to the ever-growing collection.

Wine and Art: At a wine and paint night, a group of friends decided to get creative not just with their brushes but with their wine. After a few glasses, they started using the wine itself as paint, creating abstract art pieces that were, quite literally, infused with wine. The results were surprisingly impressive, with swirls of Merlot and splashes of Sauvignon Blanc creating a unique and colorful gallery. The best part? The cleanup was easy—all you needed was a glass of wine in hand.

Wine and Movies: Looking for the perfect movie to pair with your next bottle of wine? Let me make a recommendation that's as smooth as a well-aged Cabernet: Bottle Shock. This 2008 gem tells the story of the early days of California winemaking in Sonoma County, culminating in the now-legendary Paris wine tasting of 1976—where, spoiler alert, the little guys from California took on the big names of France and, well, let's just say it's a true underdog story. With a stellar cast that includes Chris Pine, Alan Rickman, and Bill Pullman, this movie has everything you need for a cozy night in: a great storyline, beautiful cinematography, and enough wine inspiration to have you reaching for another glass. So, pop open a bottle, settle in, and enjoy the perfect blend of wine and cinema.

Wine has been a source of joy, humor, and inspiration for centuries, and as these anecdotes, quote, and fun wine activities show, it's as much about having a good time as it is about appreciating the craftsmanship behind each bottle. Whether you're laughing over a corked bottle or raising a glass to a witty toast, wine brings people together in ways that few other things can. It's a drink that encourages us to relax, to savor, and to share with others—because at the end of the day, wine is best enjoyed with a smile and good company. So, here's to the fun, the laughter, and the unforgettable moments that wine inspires. Bottoms Up!

7

Conclusion

"It's time to wine down." – **Unknown**

Wine is a celebration of life, an experience that brings people together, whether over a quiet dinner, a festive party, or a casual evening with friends. It's a drink that's been cherished by kings and commoners alike, inspiring art, music, and countless toasts over the centuries. As you continue to explore the world of wine, remember that it's not just about the labels or the vintages—it's about enjoying the moment and sharing that enjoyment with others.

So, what's next? I encourage you to take what you've learned here and put it into practice. Host a wine-tasting party with friends, visit a local vineyard, or simply open a bottle of something new and savor it with a meal. And don't be afraid to keep learning—there's always more to discover in the world of wine.

Before you go, I have one small request: If you enjoyed this book, found it informative, or had a good laugh, please consider leaving a review on Amazon. Your feedback not only helps other readers find this book, but it also supports the work that goes into creating books like this. Whether it's a few words or a detailed review, your opinion matters, and it would mean the world to me.

Thank you for joining me on this wine-filled adventure. Here's to many more glasses shared in good company and the endless joy that wine brings!

References

McDonald, J. N. (2024, April 30). 70 witty wine quotes and sayings to kick off Happy Hour. Southern Living. https://www.southernliving.com/culture/wine-quotes

The Wine Cellar Group. (2024, May 31). The best wine quotes of all time: Funny, classy, & romantic wine sayings. https://www.thewinecellargroup.com/a-collection-of-the-best-wine-quotes-of-all-time/

The Comprehensive Guide to Cinsault | Wine folly. (n.d.). Wine Folly. https://winefolly.com/grapes/cinsault/

Viognier ("Vee-own-yay") Wine Guide | Wine folly. (n.d.). Wine Folly. https://winefolly.com/deep-dive/viognier-vee-own-yay-wine-guide/

Malvasia - White Wine grape variety. (n.d.). Wine-Searcher. https://www.wine-searcher.com/grape-264-malvasia

Teroldego - Red Wine Grape Variety | Wine-Searcher. (n.d.). Wine-Searcher. https://www.wine-searcher.com/grape-484-teroldego

Bottle Shock (2008) ☆ 6.8 | Comedy, Drama. (2008, September

5). IMDb. https://www.imdb.com/title/tt0914797/

OpenAI. ChatGPT (Aug 1 version) [ENGLISHl]. Accessed [August, 2, 2024]. https://chatgpt.com/

Made in the USA
Las Vegas, NV
07 November 2024

11285041R00033